Some Quiet Place

The Loving Words of Jesus

Unless otherwise noted, Scripture quotations are from the *Revised Standard Version of the Bible*, copyright 1946, 1952, 1971 by the Division of Christian Education, National Council of Churches, and used by permission. Other Bible translations used are: the *King James Version* (KJV); *The New Testament, A New Translation* (Moffatt), copyright 1964 by James Moffatt and used by permission of the publishers, Harper and Row, Inc. and Hodder and Stoughton, Ltd.; *The New English Bible* (NEB), copyright 1961, 1970 by The Delegates of the Oxford University Press and The Syndics of the Cambridge University Press, and used by permission; *The New Testament in Modern English* (Phillips), copyright 1958, 1959, 1960 by J. B. Phillips and used by permission of the publisher, The Macmillan Company.

Photographers: Gene Ahrens, pages 10, 31, 38, 52, 58 and cover photo. Robert Cushman Hayes, pages 17, 24 and 45.

A Special Gift

_____

To

_____

_____

From

_____

_____

_____ 19 _____

Some Quiet Place

The Loving Words of Jesus

Joe R. Barnett & John D. Gipson

BROWNLOW PUBLISHING COMPANY, INC.
P. O. BOX 50545
FORT WORTH, TEXAS 76105

Brownlow Gift Books

Flowers That Never Fade
Flowers of Friendship
Flowers for You
Flowers for Mother
A Father's World
Better Than Medicine — A Merry Heart
Making the Most of Life — From A to Z
A Time to Laugh — or Grandpa Was a Preacher
Thoughts of Gold in Words of Silver
With the Good Shepherd
Living With the Psalms
The Story of Jesus
For Love's Sake
Today Is Mine
Windows
Daybreak
In His Steps
Some Quiet Place
Peace Be With You
The Fruit of the Spirit
The Greatest Thing in the World
The More Years the More Sunshine
University of Hard Knocks
The Longfellow Birthday Book
By His Side — A Woman's Place
Aesop's Fables

Contents

Preface

John had been executed. The disciples, sorrowful and frightened, retreated to Jesus' side. Staring into their weary faces He tenderly commanded, ". . .come along to *some quiet place* by yourselves, and rest for a little while" (Mark 6:31, Phillips).

How eagerly they must have anticipated these refreshing occasions when they could be alone with Jesus. John's gospel ends with the words, ". . .there are also many other things which Jesus did; were every one of them to be written, I suppose that the whole world itself could not contain the books that would be written" (John 21:25). Since exclusions from the inspired record are so mountainous and entries so carefully chosen, the choice words we have from Him must be carefully read, believed and acted upon.

During the thirty years that He lived in the mountains of Galilee He "increased in wisdom" (Luke 2:52). He emerged from these preparatory years a teacher of such merit He has for the past twenty centuries stood unchallenged as "the Master Teacher." "No man ever spoke like this man!" (John 7:46). His stamp upon history is permanent. As Emerson said, "The name of Jesus is not so much written as plowed into the history of the world."

Each of the thirty-nine devotional essays in this book has been written with the aim of pointing the reader to a particular statement of the Savior. Hope is entertained that:

> . . .like Jairus, those who come to Him bereaved will depart comforted,
>
> . . .like Mary of Magdala, those who come to Him troubled will depart in peace,
>
> . . .like Mary of Bethany, those who come to Him weeping will depart rejoicing,
>
> . . .like the woman with the issue of blood, those who come to Him trembling will depart triumphant.

If this volume contributes to such transformation its purpose will be fulfilled and the prayers of the authors answered. To that end we invite you to join us as we seek the Master in *Some Quiet Place.*

JOE R. BARNETT and JOHN D. GIPSON

Love Without Cosmetics

Proximity magnifies blemishes. The made-up movie queen may set the heart to pounding. But at close range, minus the cosmetics, she may look like something straight from Dogpatch. It's easy to "fall in love" with someone with whom you have only casual and occasional contact. That person is always seen at his best. "How wonderful it would be," we think, "to have the constant attention of such a person, so kind, understanding, considerate and charming."

But we've only seen him in his "Sunday manners." The person who *lives* with him sees the unguarded side. . .the rough edges. . .the moods, irritabilities and weaknesses. Constant contact tends to produce a "lovability gap." When the honeymoon is over and the sweet nothings have been whispered we get down to the business of living with each other. . .the hair-in-curlers, houseshoes-and-bathrobe type living.

Real love is not the condescending disdain expressed by the woman who self-righteously announced to the family, "I've prayed God for the grace to stand you all for another day." Needless to say, there was little evidence that her prayers had been answered. Those who know us at our worst and still love us exhibit rare strength. The principle applies in family, church, job or any relationship which brings us into close association. It requires no intelligence to find the faults of the person sitting at the next desk. The tendency is to neatly package his weaknesses, mark him off as incompetent or un-spiritual and entertain the self-congratulatory thought, "Thank God, I'm not like that" (Luke 18:11).

What we may fail to realize is that our feelings and expressions toward another more accurately measure our size than his. When we "size him up" we are actually whittling ourselves down to size. God is the best example of this truth. His love for us says more about *Him* than about *us.* He did not love us because *we* were worthy but because *He* was. Likewise, our sarcastic remarks about another do not advertise *his unworthiness.* . .but *our weakness.*

Remember?

"My life has been full of terrible misfortunes most of which never happened," said the great French philosopher, Montaigne. It's a terrible waste of life to spend it dreading things which are unlikely to occur. Yet, which of us has not lain awake at night conjuring up horrid pictures of what *might* happen?

One day Jesus made one of His sudden lake crossings with His disciples. So quickly did they depart they forgot to bring bread. Soon they were whispering to each other, "We have no bread." Just hours ago Jesus had miraculously multiplied meager provisions to feed a hungry multitude. Already His disciples had forgotten His power. Jesus disappointedly questioned them, "*. . .do you not remember?*" Experience had taught them nothing!

Nor can we be very critical of those ulcer-prone followers. Dealing with disciples has always been difficult. Saints are slow to comprehend. Even with the aid of inspiring Bible stories and the touch of providence in our own lives we do not remember either.

We tend to learn only half the lessons of experience. . .courting the *unpleasant* and ignoring the *pleasant*. Many a man has amassed a fortune during the past forty years who remembers nothing but the depression. Out of forty years, three tough ones. . .and they alone are remembered.

No matter how often God helps us, we're hesitant to trust Him in the next crisis. It didn't matter that God repeatedly fed and watered the Israelites. . .when they faced short rations they always started whimpering the next verse of their cynical song. Joshua saw their distressing inconsistency and chided:

> . . .you know in your hearts and souls, all of you, that *not one thing* has failed in *all* the good things which the Lord your God promised concerning you; *all* have come to pass for you, *not one of them has failed. Joshua 23:14*

And you! How many times has God failed you? "*. . .do you not remember?*"

Some Quiet Place

Hey there! What's your hurry? I've had my eye on you for a couple of weeks now, and the numerous satellites orbiting the earth are only slowpokes compared to the vapor trail you leave behind.

Time was. . .long, long ago, when you moved at a slower pace. Life was better then. But sometime in bygone days a sinister intruder slipped into your bailiwick and somehow stole something precious . . .time. And since that day I notice that you kick up dust like an overdue tornado on its way to devastation. Never mind the chest pains, the nagging ulcer, or the aching head; if we are going to do, do, do, we must go, go go!

Too often, pills wake you up in the morning and tuck you in at night. But the lines etched on your face and those steel gray hairs tell me something about inner tautness, stress and strain that even the best medicines, the best doctors can't alleviate.

Once there was a perfect man, a busy man to be sure. And he accomplished more in thirty-three years than all the octogenarians who have ever lived. Strange, isn't it, that this man even had time for little children. Though there was one interruption right after another in His work, He never seemed to be in a hurry. Maybe He just knew what was really important in life.

On one occasion this Physician wrote out a prescription for His co-workers. It said simply: "Now come along to some quiet place by yourselves, and rest for a little while."

Do you care to join me as I make my way there? Together we will pray:

> Dear Lord and Father of mankind,
>   Forgive our foolish ways;
> Reclothe us in our rightful mind,
>   In purer lives Thy service find,
> In deeper rev'rence, praise.

O Sabbath rest by Galilee,
    O calm of hills above,
Where Jesus knelt to share with thee
    The silence of eternity,
Interpreted by love!

Drop thy still dews of quietness,
    Till all our strivings cease;
Take from our souls the strain and stress,
    And let our ordered lives confess
The beauty of thy peace.

— John Greenleaf Whittier

*Now come along to
some quiet place by yourselves,
and rest for a little while.*

. . .a man shall leave his father and mother and be joined to his wife, and the two shall become one. Matthew 19:5, 6

Two or a Pair

There is an essential difference between two and a pair. The ox and the ass are two; the dog and the cat are two. . .there's no way you can arrange these in pairs. However, you can have a *pair* of mules, a *yoke* of oxen, a *team* of dogs.

With people the same holds true. *John and Judas* are two; *David and Jonathan* are a pair. John and Judas worked side by side, but a world of difference separated them. Conversely, David and Jonathan could be torn apart by danger and distance, but nothing could really separate them. . .they were forever closer than brothers.

Many things can happen to keep two from becoming a pair. Cleavage may occur because of *distance, death, social standing, or intellectual difference.* But, *moral* fracture is the worst. This is what kept John and Judas from being a pair. Similarly, moral difference gave rise to the problems between Abraham and Lot.

It can happen in the most intimate relationships when the parties do not work to keep the alliance in good repair. Jesus insisted that husband and wife should become "no longer two but one." It's beautiful beyond description when that really happens. When two become a pair the oceans of the world may separate them. Yet, they are one; a pair! Contrariwise, two may live as a family unit. . .occupy the same house, eat at the same table, share the same bed. . .yet, be oceans apart. Two, but not a pair!

What a terrible tragedy when two people walk closely together, enjoying each other's company. . .and then. . .!!! One of them becomes every day a little finer, a little kinder, a little more considerate, a little more courteous, a little more unselfish. And each day the other becomes a little more self-centered, a little less thoughtful, a little more coarse, a little more materialistic.

Jesus was not talking about sharing the same *house*, but the same *home.* It may be too sticky for our sophisticated age, but Jesus was describing *"togetherness."* The marriage ceremony does not magically eliminate collision. It requires the constantly burning fires of considerateness to melt two into a pair.

Man shall not live by bread alone, but by every word that proceeds from the mouth of God.   Matthew 4:4

Spiritual Honey

Delightful! Nourishing! Energizing! Such is the Word of God. The psalmist said, "How sweet are thy words to my taste, sweeter than honey to my mouth" (Psalm 119:103). A perfect picture. The words of the Bible mesh into an inexhaustible honeycomb, overflowing with spiritual honey.

The taste buds of every generation have been titillated by the sweetness of Scripture. When the tomb of King Tut was opened in Egypt, a supply of honey was found. After 3000 years it was still good. . .perfectly preserved. Likewise, the ancient Scriptures are ever fresh and contemporary; their message penetrates the problems of every generation. "The grass withers, and the flower falls: but the word of the Lord abides forever" (I Peter 1:24).

Spiritual *birth* comes by the Word. We are sired, ". . .not of perishable seed but of imperishable, through the living and abiding word of God" (I Peter 1:23). No other book can grip our heart, perform a miraculous metamorphosis within our soul, and present us as a beautiful trophy to the glory of God.

Once possessed, spiritual life must be continually *nourished* by the Word. Honey excels in nourishment; an energy food. No wonder God's Book is compared with honey. Peter instructs those who have been born again, "Like newborn babes, long for the pure spiritual milk, that you may grow up. . ."(I Peter 2:2). It is an inexhaustible source of spiritual supply. George Mueller said:

> The vigor of our spiritual life will be in exact proportion to the place held by the Bible on our life and thoughts. . .I look upon it as a lost day when I have not had a good time over the Word of God.

Hear it expounded regularly; study it devotionally; read it daily. How sweet it is!

What Does God Look Like?

What does God look like? Have you ever wondered about it? Of course it is well to remember that the Bible teaches that He is "invisible." This explains why Yuri Gagarin, the Russian cosmonaut, did not see God when he circled the earth in his Vostok I. Carrying his little lamp of understanding into the night, Mr. Gagarin pontifically announced that there was no one there. But how foolish it is to deny the existence of God just because He is not visible to the naked eye. After all, I have never seen a calorie, have you?

Philip, in the long ago, had just one request of Jesus: "Lord, show us the Father, and we shall be satisfied." Philip speaks for many a hungering human heart in asking for a glimpse of God. To this sincere petition Christ replies, "He who has seen me has seen the Father" (John 14:9). In Christ, God comes out of hiding; in Christ, the invisible has become visible; in Christ is a decisive revelation and clear manifestation of the Father.

Hear the declaration of Holy Scripture.

> No one has ever seen God; the only Son, who is in the bosom of the Father, he has made him known. *John 1:18*
>
> He (Christ) is the image of the invisible God. *Colossians 1:5*
>
> For it is the God who said, "Let light shine out of darkness," who has shown in our hearts to give the light of the knowledge of the glory of God in the face of Christ. *II Corinthians 4:6*
>
> He (Christ) reflects the glory of God and bears the very stamp of his nature. *Hebrews 1:3*

In Christ our wondering eyes behold: The eternal God in time. . . The invisible God in flesh. . . The infinite God in space.

Rejoice! God has graciously sent you a portrait of Himself in Christ Jesus.

Fool's Gold

Two tragedies confront a man on his journey through life — one when he wants a thing and cannot get it; the other when he gets a thing and then discovers that he does not want it.

— Elbert Hubbard

Thomas Huxley wanted a surgeon's diploma. . .until he got it. Then he suddenly realized that a surgeon's life had no attraction for him. We've known doctors, lawyers, preachers, teachers, farmers and merchants who worked hard to qualify for their occupations, only to find the appeal gone when they "arrived." Man is miserable unless he can view his work with the feeling, "To this end I was born, and for this cause came I into the world" (John 18:37).

I recall my only experience in seeking total release from home restraints. At the age of eleven I wanted freedom from parental policing. So, I announced I was leaving home. I was shocked to meet no resistance. A very wise mother told me I could have the freedom I wanted. Her only suggestion was that I wait until my father came home so he could give me some money. I would need it, she pointed out casually, to buy food, rent a room and get my clothes washed and ironed for a day or two, until I got established well enough to "make it on my own." So I waited — and thought. I was on the verge of obtaining my wanted freedom. . .and suddenly I didn't want it!

One of the most decisive lessons history has taught men is that every blessing is a curse to the person who is unready for it.

Freedom is a good thing. Those who have lived and died for freedom are the heroes of history. Yet, experience has clearly demonstrated that freedom is a good thing only for those who are prepared for it. An eleven-year-old boy is not equipped for freedom.

Power is a good thing. But power in the hands of a man (or a mob) unfitted for it leads to tyranny and disaster.

Wealth is a good thing. Yet many a man, unprepared for its administration and responsibilities, has been wrecked by sudden affluence. Perhaps this was the reason Solomon had a second thought about the inheritance he was leaving his son:

> Yea, I hated all my labour which I had taken under the sun: because I should leave it unto the man that shall be after me. And who knoweth whether he shall be a wise man or a fool?
> *Ecclesiastes 2:18, 19, KJV*

Regarding money, most men know the first of Hubbard's tragedies: wanting it and not being able to get it. And those who get it often learn Hubbard's second tragedy: having it and discovering it isn't really what they want. No man is ready for wealth unless he realizes that money cannot heal the hurt of harsh days. . .that it can't mend a broken heart or cheer a lonely soul. Nor is man equipped to handle wealth unless he understands that money is valuable only as it relates to this world. We can't "take it with us". . .and if we could it would have no purchasing power in the heavenly economy. Thus, all of man's accumulation is more worthless than "fool's gold" unless he can look back from the other side of the grave in satisfaction with the way he used it.

Camouflage

War gave us the word "camouflage." Originally it simply meant to be concealed in smoke. The big battleships, when harassed by the elusive but fatal submarines, hid themselves behind screens of impenetrable smoke. . .saved by camouflage. The technique was so effective that the tactics soon multiplied.

But, camouflage is much older than our modern wars. "Nature," says Henry Drummond, "is one vast system of imposture." Animals and reptiles have always concealed themselves with the clothing of camouflage.

People also practice camouflage. It works in two ways:

First, there are those who use camouflage to appear better than they really are. The scribes and Pharisees were masters of religious camouflage. Jesus penetrated their hypocritical hides with the stinging rebuke:

> Woe to you, scribes and Pharisees, hypocrites! for you cleanse the outside of the cup and of the plate, but inside they are full of extortion. . .you are like whitewashed tombs, which outwardly appear beautiful, but within they are full of dead men's bones and all uncleanness. So you also outwardly appear righteous to men, but within you are full of hypocrisy and iniquity. *Matthew 23:25-28*

Modern-day Pharisees still insidiously infiltrate every church. They camouflage: a vile tongue with hymns of praise, a heart of iniquity with a pious look, a covetous heart with cries of "thrift."

Second, there are those who use camouflage to appear worse than they really are. Simon Peter's heart was devoted to Jesus. But, he camouflaged that loyalty with a denial of discipleship. His twentieth century kinsmen also pretend to be irreligious when in certain company. Deep down they treasure spiritual ambitions, but camouflage them behind a facade of religious indifference.

Is your life "concealed in smoke" or is it like a "lamp. . .on a stand" that "gives light to all?"

Potential and Prayer

"Men ought always to pray," said Jesus. It is more than a privilege; it is an obligation. Evidently Jesus was aware of some power in prayer that many have overlooked, for He prayed always. Just think of it: He was without sin; the only begotten Son of God; clothed with power from on High; the only representative of perfect manhood; possessing miraculous power; yet He prayed constantly. Jesus prayed:

> after His baptism. . .
> during His personal ministry. . .
> in the garden of Gethsemane. . .
> and as He hung upon the cross.

There is no question about it. Jesus believed in prayer! To Him, God is the Father and responds as a Father to His children. In explaining this to His disciples He said, "If you then, who are evil, know how to give good gifts to your children, how much more will your Father who is in heaven give good things to those who ask him?"

Yet, despite the preaching and practice of Jesus, not many are "battering the gates of heaven with storms of prayer." We tend to cynically ask, "Why should we serve the Almighty? What is the good of us praying to him?" (Job 21:15, Moffatt). Permit Jesus to answer:

> Whatever you ask in my name, I will do it, that the Father may be glorified in the Son; if you ask anything in my name, I will do it. *John 14:13-14*

> And whatever you ask in prayer, you will receive, if you have faith. *Matthew 21:22*

> If you abide in me, and my words abide in you, ask whatever you will, and it will be done for you. *John 15:7*

No wonder Jesus said, "Men ought always to pray."

His Eye Is on the Sparrow

A man should not always expect to eat cake. Sometimes his fare will be "the bread of affliction." And in such hours it is well to remember the constant concern that a loving Heavenly Father has for His own.

Jesus put it like this:

> Are not five sparrows sold for two farthings, and not one of them is forgotten before God?

Think of it! Five sparrows for about one-fourth of a cent. Judging from the price, sparrows are not worth a great deal. But Jesus emphasizes that *not one* of them is forgotten before God. Then our Lord gently reminds us:

> Fear not therefore: *ye* are of more value than *many sparrows. Luke 12:7*

The beautiful old spiritual based on this scripture says:

> His eye is on the sparrow, and I know He cares for me.

Two Christians were once speaking of their experiences, and one said, "It is terribly hard to trust God and realize His hand in the dark passages of life." "Well, brother," said the other, "if you cannot trust a man out of your sight, he is not worth much; and, if you cannot trust God in the dark, it shows that you do not trust Him at all."

The High and Mighty

The high and mighty are everywhere. "They are so proud, so insolent, so haughty, so hollow and so loud" (Isaiah 16:6, Moffatt). They pride themselves on: beauty . . . wealth . . . social position . . . intellectual achievement . . . ability . . . race . . . spirituality . . . ad infinitum. With such an overhigh opinion of themselves, they consider others to be inferior and hardly worthy of notice.

Jesus watched the self-seekers of His day as they scrambled for the chief seats. How pitiful were their petty struggles — everyone trying to be Number One. He gave them this word of advice:

> When you are invited to a wedding reception, don't sit down in the best seat. It might happen that a more distinguished man than you has also been invited. Then your host might say, "I am afraid you must give up your seat for this man." And then, with considerable embarrassment, you will have to sit in the humblest place. . .For everyone who makes himself important will become insignificant, while the man who makes himself insignificant will find himself important. *Luke 14:8-11, Phillips*

Just as surely as thunder follows lightning, shame dogs the heels of pride. If only we could learn this — we would spare ourselves much embarrassment. Longfellow was merely repeating the unanimous verdict of human experience when he said:

> Pride goeth forth on horseback
> grand and gay,
> But cometh back on foot, and
> begs its way.

Be careful before you shout, "Glory to me in the highest! I am the greatest!" A man always pays for his pride in the coin of humiliation. The sunset of shame inevitably settles over the proud. Remember, too, that God "regards the lowly; but the haughty he knows from afar" (Psalm 138:6). Make no mistake about it, pride is one luxury we just can't afford.

In your patience possess ye your souls. Luke 21:19, KJV

Hold Your Horses

"Hold your horses," my father would say. He knew full well that I needed to gain mastery over myself — to learn to possess my own soul. For victory is impossible to the impatient. To win, one must "learn to labor and to wait."

Patience has not been prized by our generation. We are about as eager to develop patience as we are to catch the flu. It hides out among the more humble and obscure virtues. Halford E. Luccock called it the "ho hum" virtue. But Jesus recognized its tremendous importance and urged it upon his disciples.

Patience is not a passive submission to evil. Neither is it a stupid, unfeeling indifference akin to the insensibility of wood or stone.

The Greek word for patience is made up of two parts, one meaning continuance, and the other meaning submission. Patience, therefore, is the ability to hold on, to bear up under pressure. It denotes the idea of fortitude and steadfastness. "It is that quality that does not surrender to circumstances or succumb under trial."

Patience! We must have it, for provocations . . .restraints . . .injuries . . .wrongs . . .adversities and afflictions that will come. Rather than go to pieces, Jesus urges, "in your patience possess ye your souls."

Some are ardent, impulsive and adventurous, but lack the persisting patience that mocks at difficulty and commands success. They throw up their hands at the slightest obstacle and never win the victories that come to the patient. They are stymied by their own impatience.

Carey said, modestly, in his old age, when his grammars and versions of the Holy Scripture were almost a library within themselves, "I can do one thing — I can plod." Many "great works are performed not by strength, but by perseverance."

Whatever your calling, "Ye have need of patience" (Hebrews 10:36).

Give Me Tomorrow

Death is a democracy. It comes equally to us all and makes all of us equal. As Longfellow said:

> Art is long, and time is fleeting,
>   And our hearts, though stout and brave,
> Still, like muffled drums, are beating
>   Funeral marches to the grave.

Occasionally someone remarks in the spirit of Thoreau, "I'm not interested in questions on immortality. One world at a time. . .that's my motto. Do the duty that lies close at hand and don't worry about the hereafter." But this skirts the problem, for what a man believes about the hereafter affects the way he lives here. Neither does it come to grips with the age-old question, "If a man die. . .shall he live again?" As fellow travelers toward the grave, we pause. . .and ponder. . .and hope.

Philosophers often doom us to disappointment. They tend to be such a gloomy lot when faced with the question of life after death. Staring at the moving edge of time, they cringe and say:

> Where is my home? For it do I ask and seek, and have sought, but have not found it. O eternal everywhere, O eternal nowhere, O eternal in vain.
> — Nietzche
>
> There is no way out, or around, or through.
> — H. G. Wells
>
> Life is a narrow vale between the cold and barren peaks of two eternities. We strive in vain to look beyond the heights. We cry aloud, and the only answer is the echo of our wailing cry.
> — Robert Ingersol

Such words do not satisfy. They offer nothing more than a grave in a cemetery or a crypt in a mausoleum.

During the Korean struggle, the Fifth Company of Marines, with eighteen thousand men, fought against more than a hundred thousand Chinese Communists. Marguerite Higgins, the Pulitzer prize winner, reported:

> It was particularly cold — 42° below zero — that morning when reporters were standing around. The weary soldiers, half frozen, stood by their dirty trucks eating from tin cans. A huge marine was eating cold beans with his trench knife. His clothes were as stiff as a board. His face, covered with heavy beard, was crusted with mud. A correspondent asked him, "If I were God and could grant you anything you wished, what would you most like?" The man stood motionless for a moment. Then he raised his hand and replied, "Give me tomorrow."

The key to tomorrow belongs to Jesus. After demonstrating His power over death, He declared, "I am he that liveth, and was dead; and behold, I am alive for ever more, Amen; and have the keys of hell and of death" (Revelation 1:18, KJV). Triumphant in victory, He promised, "Whoever lives and believes in me shall never die." Jesus, alone, is able to give us tomorrow.

And whoever lives and believes in me shall never die.

Judge not, that you be not judged, For
with the judgment you pronounce you will
be judged. Matthew 7:1, 2

29

Put Down the Gavel

Put down the gavel! God didn't intend for us to be a judge. We must discriminate between right and wrong. . .but it is not our business to sit in judgment or to presume to allocate to others their status before God. He alone can do that. Jesus forbids our assuming a role as judge. There are two obvious reasons:

We do not know enough to judge. Unless a person has *all* the facts, and the ability to objectively analyze them, he is not in position to pass judgment. It is easier than we might think for a person to stumble into a situation so compromising that he fails to satisfactorily explain it. A man entered an office-supply store. He wanted a notebook of such size that it would fit into his inside coat pocket. In an absentminded moment he picked up a book and slipped it into his pocket to see if it would fit. Fortunately, no one saw him and he was able to replace the book as secretly as he had taken it. But suppose someone *had* seen and falsely accused him of being a thief. What defense could he have offered?

The point is made. Unless we know every detail we are in no position to judge. Long ago, Hillel, the famous Rabbi said: "Do not judge a man until you yourself have come into his circumstances or situation."

We are not good enough to judge. Jesus spoke of a man with a log in his own eye trying to extract a speck of dust from the eye of another. What right has any person to search for faults in others? There are many who claim the right to be extremely vocal in criticism while extremely exempt from action. "The stands are full of critics who fight no fights and play no ball."

The person who is unfair and severe in his judgments of others establishes a demanding standard for himself. By this irritating conduct he arouses animosity and causes others to look for his faults. One can never justifiably complain if he is judged as he judges others. We receive back from life what we pour into it. If we pour poisonous criticism into it, be sure it will spew poison back upon us.

Give up the gavel! Jesus is judge.

Existentialism and Stuff

Help! Someone please save me from contemporary philosophers. I wrestle with such words as: "existentialism," "subjectivism," "determinism," "quietism" and other grandiloquent words until I am fuzzy-headed trying to figure out what they are talking about. It's not that I am unconcerned about wisdom. I do have questions about life. I want to know why I am here and where I am going. But I haven't the strength to jump the high hurdles of many philosophical expressions. Lurking, too, in the recesses of my mind is the strong suspicion that either they do not want me to know what they are talking about, or else many of their oblique references have been born of hallucinations.

There is one thing you can say for Jesus. His language is clear. The demands may be difficult, and we may not like what He says, but at least we know what He is talking about.

And when the early Christians went out into the Roman world they had no bulging briefcases filled with memorandums to explain the complexity of the latest philosophical system. Their message was simple, "Follow Jesus!" The solution to life was in a Person rather than in a program.

Stanley Jones tells of a missionary who got lost in an African jungle. As far as the eye could see there was nothing but bush and a few cleared places. He did manage to find a native hut and a native who said he could get him out. "All right," said the missionary, "show me the way." The native said, "Walk." So they walked and hacked their way through unmarked jungle for more than an hour. The missionary got worried. "Are you quite sure this is the way? Where is the path?" The native answered, "Bwana, in this place there is no path. I am the path."

Life, for many of us, is like an African jungle. Or, to update the illustration, life is like a crowded intersection where there are no traffic lights. We become so confused that we hardly know which way to turn. Is there a way out? Listen! Above the din and confusion of our present age, a Voice can still be heard saying, "Follow me."

. . .whosoever will be chief among you, let him be your servant.
Matthew 20:27, KJV

Second Fiddles

A young preacher asked an older one to suggest a sermon series to him. "Give a series on *Second Fiddles*," the older man said. "Go through your New Testament. When you come to names like Peter, James, John and Paul, pass them by. These are *first* fiddles. But when you come to names like Phebe, Philemon, Archippus, Onesimus, Stephanas, Fortunatus, Achaicus, Amplias and Rufus, make a note of them. These are *second* fiddles. They are not born leaders; but they are superb followers."

Paul knew the value of *Second Fiddles*. One of the charms of his letters lies in the revelation of his abiding gratitude for the obscure people who cheerfully placed their services at his disposal.

Paul wanted to go to Rome. But at that time he couldn't go. So he wrote a letter. However, it was one thing for Paul to write his epistle to the Romans and quite another thing to get it into the hands of those Roman Christians. Just here Phebe enters the picture. The footnote at the end of Romans reads: "Written to the Romans from Corinth and sent by Phebe, servant of the church of Cenchrea." Phebe saw Paul's problem. . .the letter, however important and valuable, was useless unless delivered. So, traveling through hazardous country, Phebe carried Paul's letter all the way from Corinth to Rome. As she made her way along those lonely and dangerous roads, "she bore under her robe," as Renan observed, "the entire future of Christian theology." Phebe could not have written the letter; but she could deliver it to its destination.

Phebe's historic achievement in acting as Paul's postman was characteristic of her entire life. She constantly served others. She was the "helper of many" (Romans 16:2). Paul gives her a significantly beautiful title. . ."a servant of the church" (Romans 16:1). Life holds no truer worth than to be of service to somebody. Men and women who unselfishly serve shall one day hear the welcome words, "Well done, good and faithful servant!" Even amidst the glories of the Throne, the memory of service will be one of the sweetest memories of all.

Be ye therefore wise as serpents, and
harmless as doves.
Matthew 10:16, KJV

33

Wise Serpents and Harmless Doves

"Be ye therefore wise as serpents, and harmless as doves." Who, but Jesus, would utter such startling words? Doves and serpents are about as opposite as any creatures you could name. In fact, the serpent has become the symbol of the evil spirit, while the dove is the symbol of the Holy Spirit. Nevertheless, there is something about both serpents and doves that Christians should copy.

Be wise as serpents. Among the ancients the serpent was commonly regarded as the wisest of creatures. Undoubtedly this belief developed because the devil enshrined his subtlety in a serpent. Thus, since the garden of Eden the serpent has been regarded as a type of keen mind. When questioning one of my youngsters about the meaning of this Scripture, she replied, "You should be as sharp as a snake." As a Christian I have no business trying to corner the market on ignorance. There is no virtue in dullness nor sanctity in stupidity. Christ would have His disciples exercise wisdom and practice prudence.

Be harmless as doves. I have never seen a dove hurt anyone, have you? The dove has no horns with which to gore, no teeth with which to bite and no sting with which to wound. The loving nature of the dove caused it to be one of the best known and most loved of the myriads of birds of Palestine. Throughout the ages the dove has been regarded by all nations as the symbol of innocence and peace. It is unfortunate that some Christians have acquired a keenness of mind without balancing it with a gentleness of disposition. They have the wisdom of the serpent without the harmlessness of the dove.

Jesus achieved a perfect blend of these opposites and calls us to do likewise. On more than one occasion He demonstrated His wisdom and prudence. When the Pharisees tried to entangle Jesus in His talk, they asked:

> Is it lawful to pay taxes to Caesar, or not? But Jesus aware of their malice, said, "Why put me to the test, you hypocrites? Show me the money for the tax." And they brought him a coin. And Jesus said to them, "Whose likeness and inscription is this?" They said, "Caesar's." Then he said to them, "Render therefore to Caesar the things that are Caesar's, and to God the things that are God's.
>
> *Matthew 22:17-21*

Jesus knew how to behave as wisely as a serpent. But on the other hand He exhibited the harmlessness of a dove. He was skillful in confounding the clever, yet He was meek and gentle.

Beware of the person who selects either the serpent or the dove as the ideal of perfection. We must combine both concepts if we would live as Christ would have us. There is another danger. Beware, too, of those who evidently have misunderstood this Scripture and have become wise as doves and harmless as serpents.

Investing Your Money

There was a disturbing quality in the messages of Jesus that often shook His audiences with teeth-rattling abruptness. "Never man so spake," was the jolting truth which caused the powerful to fear Him. What He said often ran counter to popular concepts. So opposite to general opinion was His teaching on *giving* that even today people refuse to accept it. He said: "It is more blessed to give than to receive" (Acts 20:35). How foreign-sounding this is to our twentieth century ears. Yet, Jesus' teachings are timeless. These words were not intended only for simple, sheltered first century life. They carry equal meaning for the competitive, technological, materialistic, fast-paced twentieth century. There is *still* more happiness to be found in giving than in getting.

Spurgeon said, "A fool may make money, but it takes a wise man to spend it." The stature of a man is not revealed by only his ability to increase his financial holdings. A stronger test comes in the way he uses what he has. If God is left out of his considerations he proves himself a fool. "Thou fool!" shouted God to that man who eliminated Him from his planning (Luke 12:20). Some people become caught up in the struggle of accumulating wealth. . .and totally ignore the obligation to properly use these earnings. Money spent for eternity is money well invested. Let the moths and rust have their way with earthly treasure; our accumulations are beyond their reach when we have invested them in the Kingdom.

As the psalmist gratefully considered his God-bestowed blessings, he questioned: "What shall I render unto the Lord for all his benefits toward me?" (Psalm 116:12, KJV). God is concerned about each man's answer to that question. Jesus indicated His interest in our giving when He, ". . .beheld how the people cast money into the treasury. . ." (Mark 12:41, KJV). Seventeen of His thirty-six parables deal with stewardship. His interest quickens when we have opportunities to give, for our giving is a barometer of our love for Him (II Corinthians 8:8).

*Whoever causes one of these little
ones who believe in me to sin. . .*
Matthew 18:6

Tutors in Sin

The old man was dying. He was obviously deeply troubled. Finally, he explained why. "When we were boys at play," he said, "one day at a crossroads we reversed a signpost so that its arms were pointing in the wrong direction. I've never ceased to wonder how many people were sent in the wrong direction by what we did."

Countless people are sent in the wrong direction by improper example or advice. Jesus said: ". . .it is necessary that temptations come, but woe to the man by whom the temptation comes!" The words stress the terror of leading another into sin. Many a person sins because he has been encouraged to do so. Someone has given him a push in the direction of the forbidden.

The ancient Jews believed the most hideous sin one could commit was to teach another to sin. They argued that a man's *own* sins could be forgiven. . .that in a sense they were limited in their consequences. But, if a man taught *another* to sin, that man, in turn, might teach another. Thus, a train of sin was set in motion with no foreseeable end. . .like pushing down dominoes.

What is more terrible than to destroy another's innocence? Our text emphasizes the terror of the punishment awaiting such persons. "It would be better for him to have a great millstone fastened round his neck and to be drowned in the depth of the sea." The Jew understood the horror of that pronouncement; he hated and feared the sea. For him heaven was a place where "the sea was no more" (Revelation 21:1).

St. Bernard of Clairvaux always asked himself three questions in matters of personal indulgence:

> . . .First, Is it lawful? May I do it and not sin?
> . . .Second, Is it becoming in me as a Christian? May I do it
> and not damage my influence?
> . . .Third, Is it expedient? May I do it and not harm my
> weaker brothers?

Those are worthy questions. Attention to them would be a safeguard against leading others into sin.

Life to Gain

It's easy to quit. Anyone can do that. Maybe that's why Jesus reminds us, "By your endurance you will gain your lives." And coupled with this exhortation is the assurance:

> They that wait upon the Lord shall renew their strength; they shall mount up with wings as eagles; they shall run, and not be weary; and they shall walk, and not faint. *Isaiah 40:31*

Napoleon, it was said, had an unquestioned magic for victory, but he had no techniques for defeat. There are many people who collapse like a punctured balloon and lose heart when the slightest difficulty appears.

We must realize that the world is not arranged for the Christian to be a teacher's pet. There are times of affliction, trial and injury.

But Christianity is like grammar. It has both an active and passive voice. Long-suffering is a part of the latter. This fruit of the Spirit refuses to make an all-day sucker out of wrongs, or to gather thorns to sit on. It enables us to take a terrific strain, or to endure a thousand slings and arrows, great and small. It is the quality which enabled the apostle Paul not to be distressed when troubled, nor to be in despair when he was perplexed. He could take it all patiently.

> Lord, I would clasp thy hand in mine,
> Nor ever murmur, nor repine,
> Content, whatever lot I see,
> Since 'tis my God who leadeth me.

After all, there is life to gain.

Hidden Treasure

It was a day like any other day. John W. Huddleston was preparing to plant turnips on a parcel of ground near Murfreesboro, Arkansas. Little did he suspect that this day of planting would become a day of harvest. Yet when the sun went down that evening he was a rich man. Huddleston had discovered the first diamonds on the North American continent. And Murfreesboro in 1907 began to look like a California boomtown during Gold Rush Days. Everyone was jubilant. A treasure had been found. Gems valued up to $250,000 were soon unearthed. Since the early 1950's tourists have constantly searched the area for diamonds on a finders-keepers basis.

The subject of hidden treasure was just as exciting and fascinating during Jesus' day. In one of the Galilean's brief parables, He speaks of the value of the kingdom of heaven by comparing it to treasure hidden in a field. We see its supreme worth in the action of the finder. "He goes and sells all that he has and buys that field." Nor does he begrudge the cost involved. He considers it a priceless privilege to make such an acquisition, and purchases the field with joy.

The rewards of the kingdom are invaluable. No longer must we give anxious thought to "What shall we eat? or, What shall we drink? or, What shall we wear?" Jesus promises, "But seek first his kingdom and his righteousness, and all these things shall be yours as well" (Matthew 6:33). Coupled with this promise of earthly provision is the assurance of "all things that pertain to life and godliness" (II Peter 1:3). It is affirmed that we have "*all* spiritual blessings in heavenly places in Christ" (Ephesians 1:3, KJV).

It is one of the tragedies of our day that so many have overlooked the value of the kingdom. It is well to remember that the richest mines are often found in fields which appear most barren. But undiscerning folks will not even make an offer for the field, much less produce the purchase price. . .and, for them, the treasure remains hidden.

*. . .whatever you wish that men
would do to you, do so to them.*
Matthew 7:12

Look in the Mirror

Some persons go through life feeling cheated. A standard part of their attire is the proverbial "chip-on-the-shoulder." They make a hobby of collecting grudges, slights and insults.

Such persons have completely ignored the advice of Jesus: "Treat others as you wish to be treated!" That's the way for the good life!

We want others to be interested in us. How lonesome the cry of David: ". . .no man cared for my soul" (Psalm 142:4). Too often, David's cry becomes our own. Conversely, how heartwarming to know there are those who rejoice in our victories and sorrow in our defeats (Romans 12:15). There is a way to insure that interest. . .become interested in others! The surest way to *have* a friend is to *be* a friend (Proverbs 18:24).

We want others to look for the best in us. We don't want friends who are forever making us the object of their "mote-hunts" (Matthew 7:3). We know if others are looking for faults in us they will find them. . .because we have many. But if we want them to be kind in their judgment of us, we must be kind in our judgment of them. Remember? ". . .whatever you wish that men would do to you, do so to them." Jesus earlier said, ". . .with the judgment you pronounce you will be judged, and the measure you give will be the measure you get" (Matthew 7:1, 2).

We want others to appreciate us. The work of every person would be immeasurably easier if we expressed appreciation for that work. Jesus desired such expressions. When He had cured ten lepers and only one returned to say "thank you," Christ's response was, "Were not ten cleansed? Where are the nine?" (Luke 17:17). For a happier life, never forget the principle: if we want others to appreciate us, we must appreciate them.

Let us take this command of Christ seriously. And ever remember, what we received from others is usually just the mirrored reflection of our own conduct toward them.

The Promise of Peace

Are we drowning in a sea of troubles? Look at the chaos we reap because of man's inhumanity to man. Consider the depths of degradation in this dark world of sin. With sorrows flooding our souls, we vainly struggle to meet life's pressing duties. With Byron, the poet, we are apt to cry, "Oh, that the desert were my dwelling-place!"

How many people do you know who are suffering from some nervous disorder. . .have had a nervous breakdown. . .or, "are planning to have one" as soon as they can save up enough money to afford it?

Into such a world torn with strife came the Prince of Peace. The night that Mary brought forth her firstborn Son, shepherds abiding in the field heard an angel say, "Fear not: for behold, I bring you good tidings of great joy." And suddenly, "there was with the angel a multitude of the heavenly host praising God, and saying, Glory to God in the highest, and on earth peace, good will toward men" (Luke 2:14, KJV). Throughout His life this stranger from the shores of Galilee shone a welcome light of peace into the dark corners of the world. He reminded his disciples that whenever they entered a house they should say, "Peace be to this house" (Luke 10:5).

But eventually this hostile world hammered out the life of this peace-loving man by nailing Him to a cross. His disciples fled in fear, huddling behind a locked door. They were gripped by fear. A step on the stairs, a knock on the door might signal their arrest by emissaries of the Sanhedrin. Knowing the bitterness of the Jews, they knew their lives were in jeopardy. But suddenly. . .Jesus came into their midst breathing a benediction, "Peace be with you." Once again,

As on the Sea of Galilee,
The Christ is whispering "Peace."

No longer did they crouch in fear. No longer were their hearts troubled. They were afflicted in every way and sometimes perplexed. They were persecuted and struck down, *but they did not lose heart*. For the peace which Christ brings is superior to the storms of life. It is a peace with God and a peace within one's self. It is heaven's perfect peace.

Christ only has the answer. So into the world they went, "Preaching peace by Jesus Chrst" (Acts 10:36, KJV).

Peace I leave with you; my peace I give to you; not as the world gives do I give to you. Let not your hearts be troubled, neither let them be afraid.

In my Father's house are many rooms. . .I go to prepare a place for you. . .that where I am you may be also.
John 14:2,3

43

Just an Interruption

Many seem to die too young. Alexander the Great died at thirty-three. John Keats at twenty-six. Shelly at thirty. Byron at thirty-six.

Nor is incompleteness sensed only in those who die young. David Livingston died at sixty. In his delirium he was tortured by the thought of uncompleted tasks. "Oh, to finish my work!" he repeatedly moaned. He and many others died sighing, "So little done: so much to do!"

But man's greatest task is not to lead armies, nor to pen poems, nor to record history. His greatest work is to prepare himself internally and spiritually for a fuller and more beautiful life when this one comes to naught. This means that death in its real significance is just an interruption. Thank God for this. It is too necessary not to be true. If death ends all, there is a tragic element of waste. . .IF death ends all! But it doesn't. God doesn't spend His divine workmanship upon us only to toss us to the rubbish-heap when the work of His skillful fingers is complete.

The artist doesn't begin a canvas and unceasingly work on it until completion. He puts a few touches to it. Then, before he can go further, he must wait until those pigments are dry. We can understand the artist leaving the picture incomplete, even in the early stages of its production, if he intends to return and complete it later. Then perhaps we can understand life being prematurely interrupted by death, if He who brought it into being intends later to bring it to perfection.

Death is simply an *interruption*. Like night, it is just a parenthesis of life's activities. Victor Hugo wrote:

> I feel that I have not said a thousandth part of what is in me. When I go down to the grave I shall have ended my day's work. But another day will begin next morning. Life closes in the twilight: it opens with the dawn.

Life is an unfinished symphony, to be completed at the Great Composer's pleasure.

*Except ye. . .become as little children, ye
shall not enter into the kingdom of heaven.*
Matthew 18:3, KJV

Like Little Children

A little fellow sat on a curb. The thunderstorm was over. In his hand was a stick to which he had tied a string and a bent pin. He was fishing in the rainwater flowing down the street.

"Well, sonny, have you caught anything?" asked a passer-by.

"Not yet, sir!" he replied.

Mark that, "Not yet, sir!" It reveals dauntless certainty of success. Childhood never abandons hope. You've never met a boy who actually found a pot of gold at the end of the rainbow. But such an irrelevant observation can't keep boys from setting out in search of the dreamed-of treasure.

Remember Simeon? "The old man in the temple," you say. Not on your life! In fact, the charm about Simeon is that, though he had lived may years, he had not grown *old*. He had set his heart upon seeing "the Lord's Christ." But, unlike most of us, he never once relinquished the confident hope of witnessing the fulfillment of his dream. His expectancy never flagged.

It was an amazing achievement. Through youth, middle-age (when most give up their dreams), old age. . .he clung with unwavering tenacity to the certainty that he should not taste death until he had seen Jesus. Any person can keep hoping if nothing chills his enthusiasm. But, in Simeon's case, everything conspired to render improbable the realization of his dream. He lived through a long series of national tragedies: he saw the outbreak of civil war; he saw the coming of foreign conquerors; he saw religious decay. But he still held his faith. . .never doubted his dreams. . .certain his eyes would yet gaze upon the face of the Messiah. His was an unconquerable soul.

As we look at the wrinkled face of the aged Simeon, cradling the infant Jesus in his arms, listen to him: "Lord, now lettest thou thy servant depart in peace, according to thy word: For mine eyes have seen thy salvation" (Luke 2:29, 30, KJV). How refreshingly childlike. A little child is always confident that, come what may, some wondrous day his dream will come true. The day a person abandons hope is the day he begins to grow old.

46

Were there not ten cleansed? Where are the nine?   Luke 17:17

Forget-Me-Nots

Old Mrs. McCoy was an incurable grumbler. Nothing pleased her. One fall she had an excellent apple crop — each apple a picture of perfection. A neighbor said to her: "I know you're happy; I've heard about your wonderful apple crop." Mrs. McCoy glared at him as she replied: "I guess they'll do. . .but where's the rotten 'uns fer the pigs?" It is impossible to please some. If it rains they wish the sun would shine; if the sun shines they wish it would rain.

Ingratitude is a despicable sin. Christ cured *ten* lepers, but only *one* of them returned to say "thank you." Commenting on this poignant example of man's ingratitude, one writer said, "So often, once a man has got what he wants, he never comes back."

Because ingratitude often results from a short memory, here is a bouquet of "Forget-Me-Nots" which should be gathered by each:

Don't forget your parents. There was a time in life when we would have died if we had been neglected for a single day. And there were many years when we were totally dependent upon our parents for everything. Yet, many people forget this debt they owe, and consider the needs of their aged parents an unbearable nuisance.

Don't forget your fellowmen. At some point most of us have been helped immeasurably by a friend. He encouraged us, inspired us, motivated us, had confidence in us. . .when without it we might not have made it. At that moment we didn't think we would ever forget. But now that better days are here we have forgotten.

Don't forget God. In a time of desperate need we fervently prayed. . .God answered. . .time passed. . .we forgot.

> I'm rich! I am saved! I am happy!
> I've health and prosperity!
> I've friends! I have doors ever open!
> The Lord has been mindful of me!

Listen! "Bless the Lord, O my soul, and forget not all his benefits" (Psalm 103:2).

Verily I say unto you, Inasmuch as ye did
it not to one of the least of these, ye did it not
to me. Matthew 15:45, KJV

47

Proxies of Jesus
Scene: The Final Judgment

Christ: You are hereby condemned! I was hungry, thirsty, lonely, naked, sick and imprisoned. . .and you refused to minister to me.

Man: Wait, Lord! When did I see you in such condition? You must know I would have gladly supplied your need. In fact, I often read about Mary anointing you before burial and wished for your personal presence so I could similarly honor and refresh you.

Christ: People in sorrow, distress and poverty were all around you. Why didn't you imitate Mary's openhanded kindness by ministering to them? In neglecting *their* needs, you neglected *me*. Did you never read my words: "Inasmuch as ye did it not to one of the least of these, ye did it not to me?"

Jesus has always identified with the needy. It was His compassion toward man's need that caused Him to undertake the work of redemption. His sensitivity to our *spiritual poverty* prompted His visit to earth: ". . .though he was rich, yet for your sakes he became poor, that ye through his poverty might be rich" (II Corinthians 8:9).

Every kindness shown to the needy for His sake He accepts as if extended to Him personally (Matthew 25:31-46). Edwin Markham's poem, "How the Great Guest Came" was inspired by this passage. Markham describes Conrad, the cobbler. Conrad had a dream in which the Lord said, "I am coming your Guest to be!" So, Conrad anxiously washed the walls and shined the shelves in preparation for the Lord's visit. He set the table with milk, honey and bread. And then he waited. Soon a beggar with bruised and bleeding feet passed by. Conrad called him in and gave him a pair of shoes. Later a poor woman shuffled sadly by. Moved by her need, this kind cobbler gave her the bread. Still later there came to his door a lost, frightened child. Touched by his tears, Conrad gave him the milk and then found his parents for him. By this time the night had come. Conrad, deeply disappointed, asked the Lord why He had not kept His promise to visit his shop that day.

> Then soft in the silence a Voice he heard:
> "Lift up your heart, for I kept my word.
> Three times I came to your friendly door;
> Three times my shadow was on your floor.
> I was the beggar with bruised feet;
> I was the woman you gave to eat;
> I was the child on the homeless street."

Christ is not out of reach. He has left His proxies behind. When we minister to the needs of the poor, the afflicted, the neglected. . .He accepts our gifts as if they were placed in His own hand.

Verily I say unto you, Inasmuch as ye did it not to one of the least of these, ye did it not to me.

Man Alive!

Live! Come Alive! These are goals for which men strive. But many stumble blindly throughout the day, never quite able to discover the way. For all such weary pilgrims, Jesus opens a new vista of truth and thought when He warns that "man shall not live by bread ALONE." For man, you see, is both body AND soul. Made of the dust, he is flesh and bone; made in God's image, he is soul and spirit. The true life, life worthy of the name, life worth living, demands food for BOTH body and soul.

As surely as this earthly frame requires food, God provides. He gives fertility to flocks and field.

> Back of the loaf is the snowy flour,
>   And back of the flour is the mill,
> And back of the mill is the wheat and the shower,
>   And the sun and the Father's will.

Yet many of us remain half-starved and unsatisfied. Why? We try to live by bread alone, forgetting that somehow the soul, too, must be sustained. For unless a man's spiritual wants are supplied, he can hardly be said to live. Life is too great a thing, too Divine a gift, to be supported wholly by bread. Jesus tells us that man lives "by every word that proceeds from the mouth of God."

> A glory gilds the sacred page,
> Majestic like the sun,
> It gives a light to every age,
> It gives, but borrows none.

It is to be lamented that Bible reading and study have almost become a thing of the past. So busily engaged in reading newspapers and watching TV, we seldom pick up a copy of the Bible to pore over its pages as did our grandparents. Perhaps that is why we are starving to death.

If we were but a body, then bread would satisfy. But God made us a spirit to be fitted for the sky.

How to Make It and Lose It

"The land of a rich man brought forth plentifully; and he thought to himself, 'What shall I do, for I have nowhere to store my crops?'" Some problem. We should be so lucky! Giving additional attention to the matter, the rich man said, "I will do this: I will pull down my barns, and build larger ones; and there I will store all my grain and my goods."

The man had been pursuing an honorable calling. . .farming. . .and had obtained justifiable wealth. There's nothing wrong with that. Neither is there anything wrong with one expanding his business operation. But if you look behind the man's ACT to his ATTITUDE, you will discover a number of grievous errors.

Not one time does he think of God. He does not bless the Lord from whose hand comes all wealth. He does not ask, "What shall I render unto the Lord for all his benefits toward me?" Nor does he consider that it was God who gave him the ability to make money (Deuteronomy 8:17-19). He makes a mistake in not realizing that God made the seasons to be his servants, inspired the earth to be productive and gave this great increase. The man is a fool not to see that God is behind it all.

The rich man lives as though he were the only person in the world. He is going to build bigger barns. He will pile his goods higher and higher. He is really going to live it up. And not one time does he consider that he is a debtor. Are there none who are poorer than he? Are there no needy, no orphans? Not one tear does he see. Not one sigh does he hear. "Every man for himself" is his motto. "Soul, you have ample goods laid up for many years; take your ease, eat, drink, be merry."

"But God said to him, 'Fool! This night your soul is required of you'." At the very time he had it made, he lost it all!" "So is he who lays up treasures for himself, and is not rich toward God."

"What Will You Give Me?"

Poor Judas! He thought he was looking out for his own happiness. Dominated by desire for gain, he was willing to sell Jesus. Approaching the chief priests, Judas asked, "What will you give me to betray him to you?" The bargain was finally struck for thirty silver pieces. Judas was convinced that the only equation that really adds up in life is: Getting equals Happiness. Belatedly he discovers the error of his equation. The money was now his, but so was the misery. Filled with sorrow, he hangs himself and goes to his own place.

Straight from history comes this living testimony of the depths to which the love of money can reach and the unhappiness which follows. Why, oh why, couldn't Judas believe his Lord? After all, Jesus said, "Happiness lies more in giving than in receiving" (Acts 20:35, NEB). But Judas was not the type of man to walk by faith. He had to learn the hard way.

Is the tragedy of Judas your tragedy? How many of us, like Judas of old, are still asking, "What will you give me?" Marked by inordinate self-love and seeking, we go into a frenzy in our desire to obtain. We long for new homes, better cars, more appliances and financial security. Rule number one is, "Get the money." And rule number two is like unto it, namely, "Keep the money."

Have you ever wondered about the possibility of Jesus being right? What do you suppose it would be like to feed the hungry, clothe the naked and care for the homeless in your community?

Wanted: Men and women of faith, willing to accept the words of Jesus at face value.

The reward: Happiness.

Shut the Door

"When I've shut the door, I've shut the door!" That's how one fine Christian explained his serenity. He used to take all his troubles to bed with him. He would lie there fretting and worrying, tossing and turning. Viewed objectively, his behavior seemed absurd. He had come to his room for rest, but he was getting none. Why had he locked his office door if he was going to let the books, ledgers and order forms follow him home and haunt him? The gnawing pattern grew until it threatened to undermine his health. So, finally, he made a firm resolution, and since then, in his words, *"When I've shut the door, I've shut the door!"*

Contrast this with the young preacher who happily began his ministry with a small country church. After a while he was invited to accept the vacated pulpit of a large church. It was a tough decision. . .but at last he declined the invitation. Fine! Except that from then on when the least thing went wrong in that little church his thoughts turned to his lost opportunity. *If only he had gone! Oh, if only he had accepted that invitation!*

Later he did leave the little church to accept the invitation of a larger one. But, alas! The pressures were strong, and each day he missed something which he had loved in his Camelot. Now, when the least thing went wrong in that big church his thoughts reverted to his first ministry. *If only he had remained! Oh, if only he had never accepted this invitation!* It would have saved him immeasurable distress in both cases if he had firmly and finally *shut the doors* behind him when the decisions had been made.

We have decisions to make: to buy or refuse; to sell or hold; to go or stay; to accept or decline. Now! The decision is made. Very well, let it go at that. No need for repeated review. If the decision was sound, good. If not, no need to torture yourself by dwelling upon it. The step cannot be retraced. A wise person will shut the door!

The philosophy has been variously stated: "Live in daytight compartments". . ."Live one day at a time." Jesus said it this way: "One day's trouble is enough for one day" (Matthew 6:34, Phillips).

Double Your Joys

In a very old book I read:

> Friendship is the sweetest and most satisfactory connection in life. It has a notable effect upon all states and conditions. It relieves our cares, raises our hopes, and abates our fears. A friend who relates his successes talks himself into a new pleasure, and by opening his misfortunes leaves a part of them behind. Friendship improves happiness and abates misery by doubling our joys and dividing our griefs.

How precious, how valuable, are friends in the flesh. We simply could not get along without them. The apostle Paul knew this. He found a door open in Troas to preach the Good News of Christ, "but my mind could not rest because I did not find my brother Titus there," he said. Thus he took his leave and went into Macedonia. Years later, the apostle Paul would be led down the Appian Way to Rome. He would approach the proud city a prisoner bound with chains. But in the meantime, news of his coming reached the capital and a number of Christians set out to meet him. Some of them got as far as The Three Taverns, a stopping-place on the Appian Way about thirty-three miles from Rome; others walked ten miles farther and met him at Appii Forum. Once he had seen his brethren, "he thanked God, and took courage" (Acts 28:15).

Friends make all of the difference in the world. To feel the clasp of an outstretched hand, to walk that bridge built by love into another's presence means that the joys and sorrows of life can be shared with the knowledge that "a friend loves at all times" (Proverbs 17:17). Yet as precious as these friends are, our hearts yearn for an eternal friend; one Who in glorious, condescending love told His disciples, "I have called you friends."

> One there is, above all others,
>   Well deserves the name of Friend;
> His is love beyond a brother's,
>   Costly, free, and knows no end;
> They who once His kindness prove,
>   Find it everlasting love.

From Tranquility to Turbulence

A never-to-be-forgotten room on a never-to-be-forgotten night! What fellowship the disciples enjoyed in that Upper Room with Jesus. But it had to end. "Rise, let us go hence." These were the last five words spoken in that room that night. And they went out to persecution, martyrdom, death. . .and to kingdom-building and eternal life.

The Upper Room was a pleasant place; but its tranquility had to be disrupted. The eagle shows concern for her young, not by defending the nest, but by destroying it. A nest can become a dangerous place. Hawks and vultures see it from above; rats, weasels and snakes lurk around it. If the eaglets are too comfortable in their nest they will never attempt to fly. So the mother bird rips out the soft lining of the nest and exposes her babies' tender skin to the hard twigs beneath. They may resent the process. . .but it is for their own good.

The Upper Room experience must have been equalled only by the experience of Peter, James and John on the Mount of Transfiguration. They gazed with amazement as Moses, the Law-giver, and Elijah, the fiery representative of the prophets, conversed with the glorified Jesus. Peter could not bear the thought that this moment should prove transitory. "Lord," he cried, "it is good for us to be here. . .let us make here three tabernacles; one for thee, and one for Moses, and one for Elijah." But it could not be. At the foot of the mountain was an epileptic boy and his distressed father, sorely needing the help of Jesus. So He led His disciples down the slope to encounter the world with its aching needs. In Raphael's famous painting of the Transfiguration, the scene on the summit occupies only a corner of the picture. In the foreground is the multitude in the valley. . .the afflicted boy, helpless disciples and the anxious throng. Likewise, Jesus led His disciples out of the Upper Room because a world needed saving. The cross was waiting!

There is a longing to cling to the mountain-peak experiences. . .to erect memorials there; to remain forever in the Upper Room. We should not turn our back on these inspirational moments. But, we must also respond when He bids us rise and go hence. We must follow Him down the path of service and sacrifice. . .to Gethsemane and Calvary if necessary.

He never sends us out of the warmth of the Upper Room into the cold world alone. Only Judas left that room alone. Jesus did not say, "Go hence." He said, "Let us go hence." Let *us*! He and I together.

Holding Hands With God

The contrast of faith in Matthew 8 is striking. First, Jesus praised the faith of a centurion. His religious credentials were weak: Roman, soldier, Gentile. But he had perfect confidence in the power of Jesus. He expressed his childlike faith so convincingly that Jesus said, ". . .not even in Israel have I found such faith." On the other hand Jesus rebuked His disciples for their lack of faith. They had been eyewitnesses of His power to perform miracles. But when wind and waves began slapping at them their faith shrunk. In disappointment the Master questioned, "Why are you afraid, O men of little faith?"

Perpetual doubts harrass those who trust their own strength rather than leaning on the Lord. In the Old Testament, young David's big brothers enjoyed no victory because they expected no victory. Their faith was nil. When they heard the jeering challenges of the giant Philistine "they were discouraged and greatly afraid." But David didn't falter. The odds were no different for this ruddy boy than his brothers when he faced that giant, *except he was holding hands with God.* He expected the Lord to take a hand in the fracas. So, he taunted that swaggering giant:

> You come to me with a sword and with a spear and with a javelin; but I come to you in the name of the LORD of hosts, the GOD of the armies of Israel, whom you have defied. This day the LORD will deliver you into my hand. . .that all the earth may know that there is a GOD in Israel. . .the battle is the LORD'S. *I Samuel 17:45-47*

Faithlessness has always plagued God's people. For forty miserable years the Israelites wandered in the wilderness because of doubt. God promised them Canaan. But their "grasshopper complex" took over when they saw the giants in the land.

It's sad to see a person wandering in the wilderness of cynicism, pessimism or non-accomplishment because of failing faith. Men may fail. . .but never God. Do not forget that "what is impossible with men is possible with God" (Luke 18:27). With God as our ally nothing is too good to be true.

Failure Need Never Be Final

So you have tried and failed. The bright promise of your early day has tarnished, and those high hopes have come crashing to the ground. Visions of lost causes continue to limp before your eyes. You feel that all of life has been but a ploughing in sand, and sowing against the wind. You are almost resigned to despair.

Did you know that Michaelangelo's huge statue of David was produced from a single block of granite weighing over ten tons? This block had been rejected a century before the master sculptor used it as being unfit for a work of sculpture. Yet out of this reject he fashioned his beautiful and inspiring masterpiece. In the hands of a master, an alternative to disaster was found.

The fishermen were washing their nets. All night they had energetically toiled amid failure. Nothing had been taken. What was there to do but quit? Further effort would surely prove futile. "Not so," said Jesus to Peter. "Put out into the deep and let down your nets for a catch." So it was that the unprofitable chore was once again undertaken. . .but this time it was under the direction of the Master of men. The result? So many fish were taken that these astonished fishermen found their nets breaking. Failure had suddenly been transformed into success.

This little incident illustrates what Jesus is able to do with any situation in life. . .even the problem that grips you. Failure need never be final if Jesus is present.

So let it be in God's own might
We gird us for the coming fight.

Do not labor for the food which perishes, but for the food which endures to eternal life, which the Son of man will give to you.
John 6:27

Cotton Candy

Pink cotton candy! What a delectable food for little tow-headed boys and girls. It is as alluring and sweet to the taste as anything recently imported from dreamland. And, as my little boy said, "It makes your mouth so watery."

Parents are somewhat more discerning. Cotton candy has a terrible tendency to melt in the sun, leaving both hands and clothes somewhat on the sticky side. It is more of an illusion than a reality, for it dissolves as quickly as it is tasted.

Oh, that we could be as wise and discerning in other matters. For many of the prizes we so eagerly seek in life have about as much substance as cotton candy. These things are momentarily sweet but somehow evaporate as quickly as they are tasted. Recognizing this fact, Jesus warns, "Do not labor for the food which perishes, but for the food which endures to eternal life, which the Son of man will give you" (John 6:27).

Despite such a warning, with hearts afire and burning desire we strive to gain riches . . .fame . . .earthly enjoyment . . .glory. No effort is too great, no cost too high, no demand too rigorous. Finally out of breath and completely exhausted we achieve the desired goal. Only then, with life spent, energies depleted and health broken, do we discover to our horror that we have been laboring for that food which perishes.

But pleasures are like poppies spread —
You seize the flower, its bloom is shed;
Or like the snowflake on the river,
A moment white — then melts forever.

Just as surely as I fix my affection on this world, the time is coming when I will have nothing left but a mouth full of cotton candy.

But life does not have to end like that. There is better food. Its source is the Son of man. He alone offers us that food which endures to eternal life. . .if we want it.

He Believes in You

"I've committed so many sins God could never forgive me," the letter began. Preachers often receive such letters from those who do not comprehend the forgiving power of God. Thousands of people live daily under the crush of past sins; slaves of the irrevocable past. Oh, how they need an encounter with Jesus! Our text speaks of a woman, guilty of adultery, who found Jesus an understanding counselor, anxious to help. After listening to the accusations of her rude companions and abruptly dismissing them, He said to her, "Neither do I condemn thee: go, and sin no more." No story more clearly reveals the compassion of Christ. He was not soft toward sin. He was not condoning this sinful woman's wrongs. But He was giving her another chance. Jesus' attitude toward this sinner reveals two encouraging things:

His confidence in human nature. Don't give up on yourself too soon — Jesus believes in you. Many would have marked this sinful woman off as hopeless and unworthy of help. But not Jesus! He had faith that this flagrant sinner could, with His help, become a saint. He believed in a handful of common fishermen so completely that He placed the future of His kingdom in their hands. He believed in "the chief of sinners," and helped him become a chief of saints. Jesus didn't blast men with the accusation that they were miserable sinners when they already were painfully aware of it. Instead, He inspired them with the happy truth that they were potential saints.

His offer of another chance. Someone has written:

> How I wish that there was some wonderful place
>   Called the Land of Beginning Again,
> Where all our mistakes and all our heartaches
>   And all our poor selfish grief
> Could be dropped like a shabby old coat at the door
>   And never put on again.

Jesus offers the gospel of the second chance. He is intensely interested not only in what a person *has been*, but also in what a person *can be.* He never indicates that what one has done doesn't matter. . .broken laws always matter. But Jesus is more interested in a man's *future* than his *past.* He challenged the adulterous woman to live better in the future. He didn't say, "It's all right." He said, "It's all wrong! You have sinned. Go out and prove you can do better. Sin no more."

One cannot live productively in the *present,* nor effectively face the *future,* if his thoughts are buried in the *past.* Moaning over that which cannot be changed is a wasteful exercise. Be thankful that you have been given time to restructure your life. Do not despair; think what you can become with God's help. He believes in you!

Neither do I condemn thee: go, and sin no more.

Stay With It

"Blood, sweat and tears!" That's what Churchill offered his country after Dunkirk. This is not the ordinary politician's way of winning adherents. But, perhaps Churchill learned his honesty from Jesus. Jesus did not hesitate to tell men what to expect when they followed Him:

> I send you out as sheep in the midst of wolves. . .they will deliver you up to councils, and flog you in their synagogues, and you will be dragged before governors and kings. . .and you will be hated. . . *Matthew 10:16, 17, 22*

That's harsh language for modern ears. We prefer the part where Jesus says, "Come. . .and I will give you rest. . .my burden is light" (Matthew 11:28, 30). We want that! We want it without cost. And we want it before the sun goes down.

But we can't have it that way. Jesus' religion tests a man's fortitude; gives his character a chance to display strength. The greater the difficulties we encounter in our struggle for victory, the greater our satisfaction will be when we have surmounted them. A man may be *enjoyed* for his jovial nature when health and wealth are his. . .but a man is *admired* for his courage in facing adversity.

> . . .statues are not erected to honor the clean-up detail;
>   but to soldiers who risk life.
> . . .Purple Heart medals are not awarded to parade units;
>   but to men who dare death for a cause.
> . . .the apostles are not admired for their affluence; but
>   for their courage.

Not cushions but obstacles. . .not ease but difficulties make successful people. "Fortitude is the diet of champions."

But I say to you, Love your enemies.
Matthew 5:44

What the World Needs Now

"Love your enemies," said Jesus. Who else would make such a statement? Only Jesus would dare utter the words and expect men to obey them. Most of us are ready to slap down our enemies as soon as they get in our way. But to love them?. . .that's another story. As demanding and difficult as this duty is, it is exactly what Jesus requires. He is neither speaking of the impossible nor dealing in nonsense.

Not only did Jesus *preach* such love; He *practiced* it. To survey the cross is to see love personified.

> See, from His head, His hands, His feet,
> Sorrow and love flow mingled down;
> Did e'er such love and sorrow meet,
> Or thorns compose so rich a crown?

Modern psychologists stress the need for loving; it is a question of "Love or Perish." They warn that we can't live with hatred without damaging our own personality, for enmity is an enemy of the soul. Contemporary man is just now discovering the importance of the principle commanded by Christ centuries ago.

Love is still the most impelling force in the universe. I have always enjoyed that legendary conversation between the Wind and Sun. They argued about which of them was the more powerful. Spying a man on earth wearing an overcoat, they conceived the idea of testing their respective power by seeing which of them could the more quickly make him remove his coat. The wind began the contest, blowing his ferocious and icy blasts, only causing the man to hug himself tighter in his warm wrappings. Then the sun started, pouring down his rays of heat, with the result that soon, first the gloves, then the scarf, came off — and then the overcoat. The sun always wins.

The trouble with the world today is that it is choking and dying because of hate and revenge. Only Jesus holds forth an adequate remedy. . .if we will accept it. "What the world needs now is love, sweet love."